Monster Fliers

From the Time of the Dinosaurs

Written by **Elizabeth MacLeod**

Illustrated by **John Bindon**

Kids Can Press

Zoom!

They soared over prehistoric forests. They swooped down to snatch fish out of lakes and oceans. Monster fliers ruled the sky, while the dinosaurs roamed the land below.

Many of the ancient fliers in this book are pterosaurs — flying reptiles that lived at the same time as dinosaurs. Others are long-ago birds. And one is a dromaeosaur, a small, fast dinosaur that walked on two legs and could fly.

Flying made it easy for these creatures to find a mate and hunt dinner. They could cover a larger area by flying than by walking.

Small pterosaurs flapped their wings to fly, the same way small birds fly today. Pterosaurs with huge wings soared through the sky, like modern big-winged birds. They rode air currents to get around. Like today's birds, pterosaurs had lightweight bones.

Get ready to meet some of the largest creatures ever to fly — and some of the weirdest looking!

Early Flier

Eudimorphodon (you-di-MOR-foe-don) was one of the earliest pterosaurs (flying reptiles). Its wings were made of light, stretchy skin. A long, stiff tail with a flap at the end helped keep it steady as it flew.

See the claws halfway along its wings? Those are this pterosaur's first three fingers. Its fourth finger stretches from there to its wing tip. (Unlike you, *Eudimorphodon* had no fifth finger.)

This pterosaur ate fish. The long, sharp teeth at the front of its mouth grabbed the fish, while the short back ones held on to it.

Big Head

The head of this *Dimorphodon* (di-MOR-foe-don) may look big and heavy, but the bones of its skull were full of hollow spaces.

Like most pterosaurs, *Dimorphodon* had legs that sprawled out sideways. Although its long tail helped balance its large head, it was probably very clumsy on land. To keep safe, pterosaurs such as *Dimorphodon* probably stayed off the ground. They would hang from cliffs or tree branches with their strong claws.

Toothy Pterosaur

Ctenochasma (TEN-o-KAS-ma) was born with about 60 teeth — and kept growing more! New teeth appeared at the front of its jaw until it had as many as 400. When scientists first found this pterosaur's bones, they thought they had found an ancient crocodile.

Ctenochasma likely waded in shallow water, scooping up tiny animals and water in its bill. The water drained out between its teeth, leaving the small creatures behind.

Tiny Terror

One of the smallest pterosaurs was *Anurognathus* (a-NOOR-og-NATH-us). From wing tip to wing tip, it was only about the length of your arm. Its body was about the size of a softball.

Anurognathus had short, peglike teeth that it may have used to eat insects. It must have been a good flier to catch them, swooping and darting and making quick turns.

Like some birds today that hitch rides on elephants, *Anurognathus* may even have ridden on the backs of large dinosaurs, eating insects the dinosaurs stirred up as they walked.

Thin-Winged Hunter

Scaphognathus (ska-FOG-nath-us) was a small pterosaur. It had few teeth and a rounded beak, not a pointed one like many pterosaurs.

Experts aren't sure if *Scaphognathus* ate insects or fish. It may even have eaten small animals that lived on land. This pterosaur's big brain and sharp eyesight probably made it a good hunter.

Scaphognathus had a flap of skin at the tip of its long, bony tail. This flap kept it steady as it flew. Its long, thin wings helped it fly great distances.

Crest Heads

Scientists think *Gallodactylus* (GALL-o-DACK-til-us) and *Germanodactylus* (jer-MAN-o-DACK-til-us) were the first pterosaurs with head crests.

Gallodactylus (below) had a head crest that was small and might have been brightly colored. It may have used its crest to signal to another *Gallodactylus* and to attract a mate.

Notice the teeth at the tip of its long, narrow bill? They are perfectly positioned to grab fish, this creature's favorite meal.

Germanodactylus was a pterosaur about the size of a seagull. Its straight head crest may have kept its head from wobbling as it skimmed the water to grab dinner.

Strong claws on its wings probably helped it climb trees. The claws on its feet may have let it cling to cliffs or hang upside down from branches.

Furry Flier

Usually scientists find only the bones of ancient animals. But *Sordes* (SORE-dees) also left an imprint of its skin. This print showed that this little pterosaur had thick hair on its body to keep warm.

Sordes had big eyes and nostrils but tiny teeth. It ate small creatures, such as insects.

Notice how its wings are attached to its legs? That probably made it difficult for *Sordes* to walk on two legs, the way birds do. So, like many small pterosaurs, this little flier walked on four legs.

Well-Known Pterosaur

Because so many fossils have been found of *Pterodactylus* (tare-o-dack-TIL-us), it's one of the best-known flying reptiles.

This tiny flier was one of many pterosaurs that soared over lagoons, diving down to scoop up fish. Like a pelican, *Pterodactylus* tucked its dinner into a pouch in its throat, then headed for land to eat its meal.

World's Oldest Bird

Like today's birds, *Archaeopteryx* (ark-ee-OP-ter-icks) had feathers and hollow bones. But, unlike modern birds, it had sharp teeth, clawed fingers on its wings and a long, bony, dinosaurlike tail.

Archaeopteryx may have glided from tree to tree or leapt and run along the ground. See the three sharp, curved claws near the end of its wing? These claws and the claws on its toes probably helped it climb trees.

Strange Bills

Imagine a mouth crammed with about a thousand bristlelike teeth. *Pterodaustro* (tare-o-DAW-stro) had one of the strangest, longest bills of any pterosaur. When this monster flier shut its mouth, its long lower teeth stuck out around its bill.

To get its dinner, *Pterodaustro* stood in water. It skimmed its bill over the surface like a net. When it raised its head, the water flowed out. Small creatures were trapped in its bill, and *Pterodaustro* gulped them down. The tiny teeth in its upper jaw helped chop up larger food.

Dsungaripterus (jung-gah-RIP-tare-us) had a pointed bill that was perfect for prying open crabs and other shellfish. It had no front teeth and only bony knobs at the back of its jaw. The knobs helped it crush the shells of its dinner so it could eat the tasty bits inside.

Tip to tip, this pterosaur's wings were about as long as two ten-year-olds lying head to head. These large, lightweight wings let *Dsungaripterus* travel long distances, gliding on the breezes.

Four-Winged Flier

Microraptor (MY-crow-rap-tore) was a type of dinosaur known as a dromaeosaur, which means "running lizard." See the long feathers on its legs? They gave *Microraptor* a second set of wings. But these double wings may have kept it from running fast. To be safe, it may have lived in trees, gliding from branch to branch.

Microraptor was a hunter. It used its claws for slashing and stabbing.

Early Bird

Confuciusornis (kon-FEW-shi-SORE-nis) was one of the first birds to have no teeth. It was also the first bird to have a tough beak, like a modern bird.

Except for the claws halfway along its wings, *Confuciusornis* looked like a bird you might see today. Those claws helped it walk and climb.

Some of these birds — perhaps the males — had long tail feathers. Others had short tails.

Watery Flier

The stubby wings of *Hesperornis* (HES-per-OR-nis) were no use for flying through the air. Instead, *Hesperornis* used its feet to propel itself through the water when hunting fish and squid.

The legs of this prehistoric bird were set far back on its body. That gave it a sleek, streamlined shape for swimming. But setback legs made walking on land very awkward. *Hesperornis* may have pushed itself along the ground on its belly.

Bulgy Bill

You might think the big bump on the beak of *Tropeognathus* (TROPE-ee-og-nath-us) would make flying tough. Actually, the crest helped this pterosaur move smoothly — through water!

Tropeognathus flew over water and dipped in the tip of its beak to catch fish. Its beak bump helped it cut through the water and keep its head steady. Its skull was 60 cm (2 ft.) long — about the length of your arm.

The Biggest Flier Ever

There has never been another flier as huge as *Quetzalcoatlus* (KWET-zal-KWAT-luss). This pterosaur had the wingspan of a small airplane. It may have launched itself off cliffs or hills, then glided on air currents.

Its long neck may have helped *Quetzalcoatlus* plunge its head into shallow streams and pools to grab crabs or other creatures. It may even have eaten dead animals.

Killer Crane

Known as the Terror Bird or Killer Crane, *Titanis* (tie-TAN-iss) lived just after dinosaurs became extinct. It is the largest bird of prey ever — that means it is the biggest of all the birds to hunt animals. It would have been too tall to stand in your bedroom.

   Titanis couldn't fly. Instead, it may have crept up on giant armadillos and antelope-like creatures. Then it dashed forward, grabbing with its claws. This bird's monstrous beak could slice through tough flesh, but it often gulped down its prey whole.

World's Biggest Bird

Long after the dinosaurs had left the earth, *Argentavis* (ar-jen-TAVE-is) glided through the sky. *Argentavis* was bigger than any other bird, ancient or modern. From wing tip to wing tip, it stretched longer than a minivan. Its feathers may have been as long as you are tall.

Flapping those huge wings used lots of energy, so *Argentavis* usually beat its wings only to take off or change direction.

HOW BIG WERE THEY?

This scale diagram shows how big the fliers in this book are compared to one another — and to the kids shown here. You can also find out when each one lived.

Eudimorphodon
Lived 220 million years ago

Scaphognathus
Lived 150 million years ago

Archaeopteryx
Lived 150 million years ago

Dimorphodon
Lived 205 million years ago

Gallodactylus
Lived 150 million years ago

Pterodaustro
Lived 140 million years ago

Ctenochasma
Lived 150 million years ago

Germanodactylus
Lived 150 million years ago

Dsungaripterus
Lived 130 million years ago

Anurognathus
Lived 150 million years ago

Sordes
Lived 150 million years ago

Pterodactylus
Lived 150 million years ago

Microraptor
Lived 125 million years ago

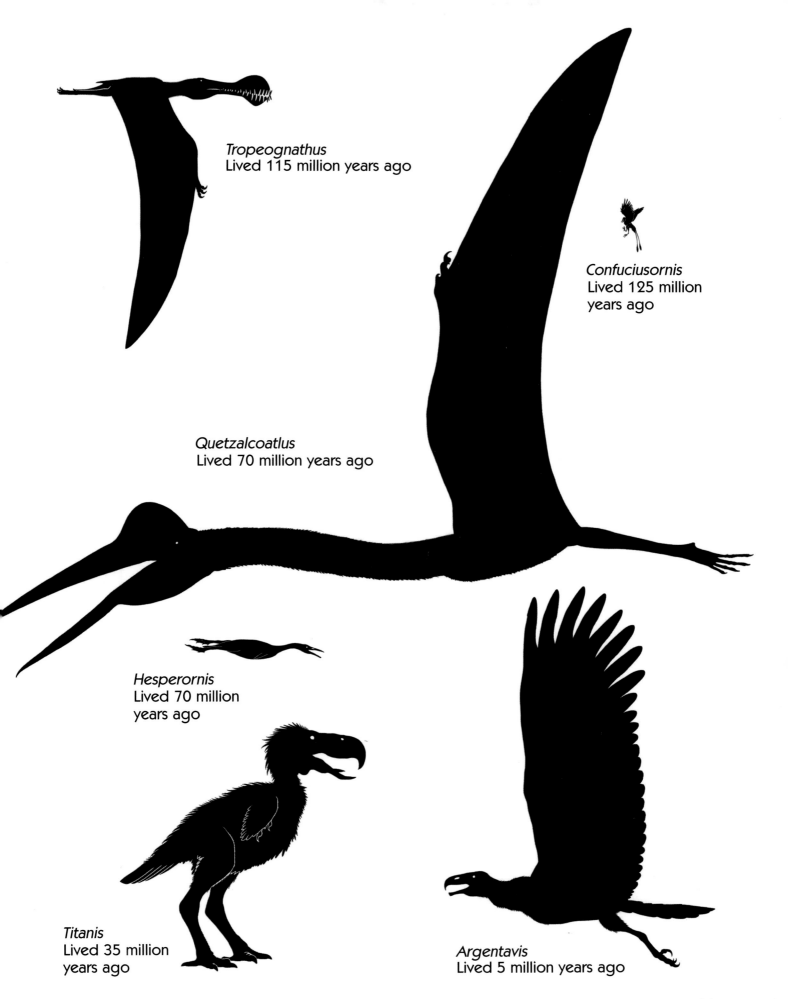

Tropeognathus
Lived 115 million years ago

Confuciusornis
Lived 125 million
years ago

Quetzalcoatlus
Lived 70 million years ago

Hesperornis
Lived 70 million
years ago

Titanis
Lived 35 million
years ago

Argentavis
Lived 5 million years ago

With much love to the pterribly pterrific Addie and Jake — EM
To Frances for her love and support — JB

Text © 2010 Elizabeth MacLeod
Illustrations © 2010 John Bindon

Acknowledgments
This book was definitely a team effort — and what a team! Many, many thanks to
the expert consultant Chris McGowan, incredible artist John Bindon, amazing designer
Julia Naimska and fabulous editor Val Wyatt. And love and thanks always to Paul.

Consultant
Dr. Chris McGowan, Curator Emeritus, Vertebrate Paleontology, Royal Ontario Museum

Kids Can Press acknowledges the financial support of the Government of
Ontario, through the Ontario Media Development Corporation's Ontario Book Initiative;
the Ontario Arts Council; the Canada Council for the Arts; and the Government
of Canada, through the BPIDP, for our publishing activity.

Published in Canada by
Kids Can Press Ltd.
29 Birch Avenue
Toronto, ON M4V 1E2

Published in the U.S. by
Kids Can Press Ltd.
2250 Military Road
Tonawanda, NY 14150

www.kidscanpress.com

Edited by Valerie Wyatt
Designed by Julia Naimska
Printed and bound in Singapore

This book is smyth sewn casebound.

CM 10 0 9 8 7 6 5 4 3 2 1

Library and Archives Canada Cataloguing in Publication

MacLeod, Elizabeth
Monster fliers : from the time of the dinosaurs / written by
Elizabeth MacLeod ; illustrated by John Bindon.

ISBN 978-1-55453-199-8 (bound)

1. Pterosauria—Juvenile literature. 2. Dinosaurs—Juvenile literature. 3. Birds, Fossil—Juvenile
literature. I. Bindon, John II. Title.

QE861.5.M335 2010   j567.918   C2009-903364-X

Kids Can Press is a *Corus*™ Entertainment company